My Wisdom Book

Everyday Shlokas, Mantras, Bhajans and More

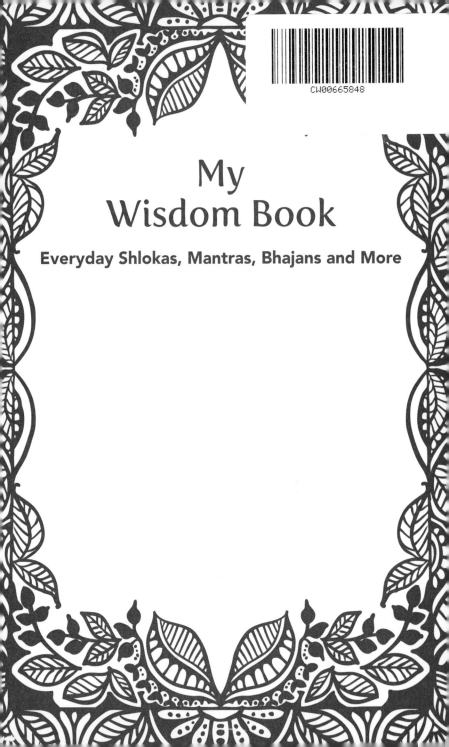

RED PANDA

First published by Red Panda, an imprint of Westland Publications Private Limited, in 2021

1st Floor, A Block, East Wing, Plot No. 40, SP Infocity, Dr MGR Salai, Perungudi, Kandanchavadi, Chennai 600096

ISBN: 9789391234263

Book design by New Media Line Creations, New Delhi 110 062

Printed at Thomson Press (India) Ltd.

MY WISDOM BOOK

Everyday Shlokas, Mantras, Bhajans and More

Swami Mukundananda

Illustrated by
Rayika Sen

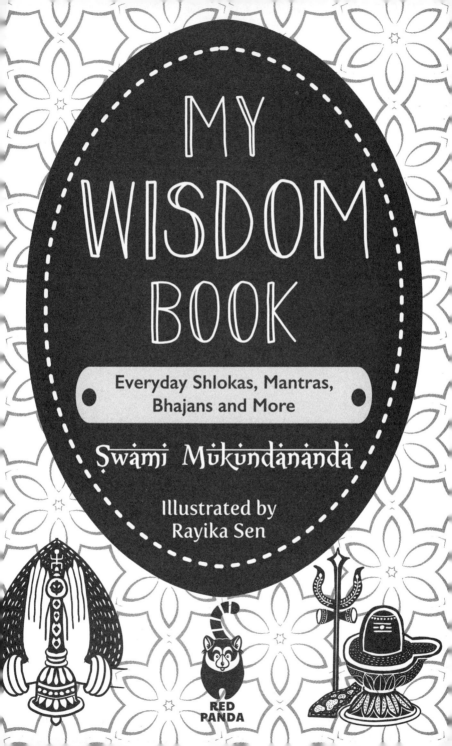

RED PANDA

Contents

Introduction

God loves a simple, childlike heart. And it is important to nurture that innocent little heart with wisdom and values. The beliefs inculcated in children at a young age enable them to paint their future on the canvas of life. The colours they choose depends on the values taught by their teachers and parents.

The most crucial part of revealing wisdom is to impart the right knowledge from the right source. And there is no better or more authentic source than Vedic philosophy.

The Vedas are eternal. They were manifested with the breath of God. Their infinite wisdom was passed down through generations. Yet, this priceless knowledge is incredibly relevant even today.

For this book, we have handpicked some of these gems of wisdom, which can be instrumental in forging a child's character. Just like wet clay that can be moulded into any shape, we hope this book will shape children's hearts and personalities.

The beauty of the Sanskrit language is that it contains immense knowledge in just a few words. *My Book of Wisdom* is a consolidation of key shlokas and mantras that are easy to comprehend, remember and implement.

Reciting the shlokas and mantras daily helps children develop their EQ (emotional quotient) and SQ (spiritual quotient), along with IQ (intelligence quotient). Research proves that it also helps improve a child's concentration and cognitive power. It even enhances their pronunciation, helping them become better communicators.

Juniors

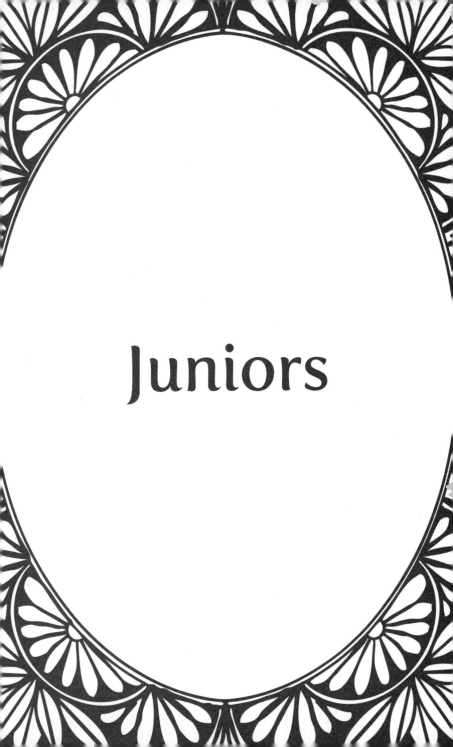

Shlokas

The Guru

Respect for the Teacher (Guru Vandana)

गुरुर्ब्रह्मा गुरुर्विष्णुः गुरुर्देवो महेश्वरः।
गुरुः साक्षात् परब्रह्म तस्मै श्रीगुरवे नमः॥

gurur-brahmā gurur-viṣhṇuḥ gurur-devo maheśhvaraḥ
guruḥ sākśhāt para brahma tasmai śhrī-gurave namaḥ

We respect our teacher as we respect Lord Brahma. We respect our teacher as we respect Lord Vishnu. We pay respects to our teacher as we would to Lord Shiv. We see our teacher as a manifestation of the Supreme Divine.

Daily Shlokas

Upon Waking Up

कराग्रे वसते लक्ष्मीः करमध्ये सरस्वती।
करमूले तु गोविन्दः प्रभाते करदर्शनम्॥

karāgre vasate lakṣhmīḥ karamadhye sarasvatī
karamūle tu govindaḥ prabhāte karadarśhanam

Early in the morning, we look at our palms. Goddess Lakshmi resides at the top of our palms, Goddess Saraswati resides at the centre of our palms and Lord Krishna resides at the base of our palms.

Before Stepping Out of Bed

समुद्र-वसने देवि पर्वत-स्तन-मण्डिते।
विष्णु-पत्नि नमस्तुभ्यं पाद-स्पर्शं क्षमस्व मे॥

samudra-vasane devi parvata-stana-maṇḍite
viṣhṇu-patni namastubhyam pāda-sparśham kṣhamasva me

We ask for forgiveness from Mother Earth (the wife of Lord Vishnu) for placing our foot upon Her. She is the bearer of elegant waters and mighty mountains.

While Bathing

ॐ गङ्गे च यमुने चैव गोदावरि सरस्वति।
नर्मदे सिन्धु कावेरि जलेऽस्मिन् सन्निधिं कुरु॥

oṁ gaṅge cha yamune chaiva godāvari sarasvati
narmade sindhu kāveri jale'smin sannidhim kuru

Om! We think of the water used for cleansing our body as a blend of the waters from Ganga, Yamuna, Godavari, Saraswati, Narmada, Sindhu and Kaveri (the seven holy rivers).

Prayers to the Lord

त्वमेव माता च पिता त्वमेव
त्वमेव बन्धुश्च सखा त्वमेव।
त्वमेव विद्या द्रविणं त्वमेव
त्वमेव सर्वं मम देव देव॥

tvam-eva mātā cha pitā tvam-eva
tvam-eva bandhuśh-cha sakhā tvam-eva
tvam-eva vidyā draviṇam tvam-eva
tvam-eva sarvam mama deva deva

We love God as we love our mother. We love Him as we love our father. We love God as we love our relatives and friends. We love the Almighty as much as we love our wealth and knowledge. We inculcate love towards God as if He were our everything.

Prayers to the Lord

वसुदेवसुतं देवं कंसचाणूरमर्दनम्।
देवकीपरमानन्दं कृष्णं वन्दे जगद्गुरुम्॥

vasudeva-sutam devam kansa-chāṇūra-mardanam
devakī-paramānandam kṛiṣhṇam vande jagadgurum

We bow down to Shri Krishna, son of Vasudev and demolisher of the demons Kansa and Chanur. He is the reason for Mother Devaki's everlasting bliss and the Supreme Master of the world.

Before Starting a New Endeavour

वक्रतुण्ड महाकाय सूर्यकोटि समप्रभ।
निर्विघ्नं कुरु मे देव सर्वकार्येषु सर्वदा॥

vakra-tuṇḍa mahā-kāya sūrya-koṭi samaprabha
nirvighnam kuru me deva sarva-kāryeṣhu sarvadā

We pray to Lord Ganesh, the one who possesses a twisted trunk, a huge body, and whose brilliance is equivalent to a million suns. His grace will eradicate all obstacles that may come our way.

Before Sitting Down to Study

ॐ सरस्वति नमस्तुभ्यं वरदे कामरूपिणि।
विद्यारम्भं करिष्यामि सिद्धिर्भवतु मे सदा॥

om̃ sarasvati namastubhyam varade kāma-rūpiṇi
vidyārambham kariṣhyāmi siddhir-bhavatu me sadā

Om! We pray to Mother Saraswati, the goddess of learning, asking Her for a boon. As we begin our studies, may She always reward our efforts.

Before Eating

ब्रह्मार्पणं ब्रह्म हविर्ब्रह्माग्नौ ब्रह्मणा हुतम्।
ब्रह्मैव तेन गन्तव्यं ब्रह्मकर्मसमाधिना॥

brahmārpaṇam brahma havir brahmāgnau brahmaṇā hutam
brahmaiva tena gantavyam brahma-karma-samādhinā

For those completely absorbed in God-consciousness, the offering is Brahman (the Divine), the ladle with which it is offered is Brahman, the act of offering is Brahman and the sacrificial fire is also Brahman. Such people, who view everything as God, attain Him easily.

While Lighting the Lamp

शुभं करोति कल्याणं आरोग्यं धनसम्पदा।
शत्रुबुद्धिविनाशाय दीपज्योतिर्नमोऽस्तुते॥

śhubham karoti kalyāṇam ārogyam dhana-sampadā
śhatru-buddhi-vināśhāya dīpa-jyotir-namostute

We offer our respects to the Supreme Lord present in the light of the lamp. The Lord will destroy the enemies within our mind (like anger, greed, pride and jealousy) and bring well-being, prosperity, good health and wealth.

Bedtime Prayer

रामस्कन्दं हनुमन्तं वैनतेयं वृकोदरम्।
शयने यः स्मरेन्नित्यं दुःस्वप्नं तस्य नाशयति॥

rāmaskandam hanumantam vainateyam vṛikodaram
śhayane yaḥ smarennityam duḥsvapnam tasya nāśhayati

Before we go to sleep, we fill our mind with thoughts of Shri Ram, Lord Karthikeya, Lord Hanuman, Garud and the mighty Bhimsen. May their grace protect us and prevent us from having nightmares.

Lord Ganesh

Mooshika Vahana

मूषिकवाहन मोदकहस्त चामरकर्ण विलम्बितसूत्र।
वामनरूप महेश्वरपुत्र विघ्नविनाशक पाद नमस्ते॥

mūṣhikavāhana modakahasta chāmarakarṇa vilambitasūtra
vāmanarūpa maheśhvaraputra vighna-vināśhaka pāda namaste

We offer our respects at the feet of Lord Ganesh, the destroyer of all obstacles. His vehicle is the mouse and He holds the modak in His hands. He has huge ears that resemble a fan. He is stout and wears a sacred thread around His body. He is worshipped as the son of Lord Shiv.

Ekadantaya Vidmahe

एकदन्ताय विद्महे।
वक्रतुण्डाय धीमहि।
तन्नो दन्तिः प्रचोदयात्।

ekadantāya vidmahe
vakratuṇḍāya dhīmahi
tanno dantiḥ prachodayāt

We pray to Lord Ganesh, who possesses a majestic elephant head adorned with a single tusk, to illuminate our intellect with divine knowledge. We pray to the one with a curved trunk that our mind may always meditate upon Him.

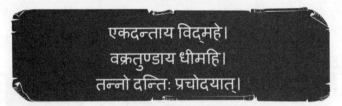

Lord Krishna

Achyutam Keshavam

अच्युतं केशवं रामनारायणम्
कृष्णदामोदरं वासुदेवं हरिम्।
श्रीधरं माधवं गोपिकावल्लभम्
जानकीनायकं रामचन्द्रं भजे॥

achyutam keśhavam rāma-nārāyaṇam
kṛiṣhṇa-dāmodaram vāsudevam harim
śhrīdharam mādhavam gopikā-vallabham
jānakī-nāyakam rāmachandram bhaje

We sing the glories of Shri Krishna. He is infallible. He is the killer of Keshi, the demon. Krishna is all attractive. He is known as Vasudev, Damodar, Hari, Sridhar, Madhav, Ram and Narayan. In the form of Lord Krishna, He is the beloved of the gopis. In the form of Lord Ram, He is the beloved of Mother Sita.

Mookam Karoti Vachalam

मूकं करोति वाचालं पङ्गुं लङ्घयते गिरिम्।
यत्कृपा तमहं वन्दे परमानन्द-माधवम्॥

mūkam karoti vāchālam paṅgum laṅghayate girim
yatkṛipā tamaham vande paramānanda-mādhavam

We bow down to Shri Krishna (Madhav), the ocean of Supreme Bliss, with utmost respect. By His causeless grace, a dumb person can speak words of wisdom and a lame person can cross a mighty mountain.

Lord Ram

Ramaya Ramabhadraya

रामाय रामभद्राय रामचन्द्राय वेधसे।
रघुनाथाय नाथाय सीतायाः पतये नमः॥

rāmāya rāmabhadrāya rāmachandrāya vedhase
raghunāthāya nāthāya sītāyāḥ pataye namaḥ

We offer our salutations to the great Lord Ram, who is also known as Ramabhadra and Ramachandra. He is famous in the world as Raghunath, the Supreme Master, and the husband of Sita.

Shri Rama Rama Rameti

श्री राम राम रामेति रमे रामे मनोरमे।
सहस्रनाम-तत्तुल्यं राम नाम वरानने॥

śhrī rāma rāma rāmeti rame rāme manorame
sahasranāma-tattulyam rāma nāma varānane

We chant the names of Lord Ram, absorbing our mind completely in Him. We revere His name, thinking of it as equivalent to a thousand names of Lord Vishnu.

Lord Hanuman

Manojavam Maruta Tulya Vegam

मनोजवं मारुततुल्यवेगं जितेन्द्रियं बुद्धिमतां वरिष्ठम्।
वातात्मजं वानरयूथमुख्यं श्रीरामदूतं शरणं प्रपद्ये॥

manojavam mārutatulya-vegam jitendriyam buddhimatām varişhṭham
vātātmajam vānara-yūtha-mukhyam śhrī-rāma-dūtam śharaṇam prapadye

We surrender ourselves at the lotus feet of Lord Hanuman, who is as nimble as the mind and can travel at the speed of the wind. He has mastered the control of His senses. He is supremely intelligent and wise. He is the son of the wind god and the leader of the monkey army. He is the messenger of the all-powerful Shri Ram.

Buddhir Balam Yasho Dhairyam

बुद्धिर्बलं यशो धैर्यं निर्भयत्वं अरोगताम्।
अजाड्यं वाक् पटुत्वं च हनुमत् स्मरणात् भवेत्॥

buddhirbalam yaśho dhairyam nirbhayatvam arogatām
ajāḍyam vāk paṭutvam cha hanumat smaraṇāt bhavet

We meditate upon Lord Hanuman so that He may bestow upon us wisdom, strength, fame, forbearance, fearlessness and good health. He will help us overcome laziness and develop excellent communication skills.

Lord Vishnu

Shantakaram Bhujagashayanam

शान्ताकारं भुजगशयनं पद्मनाभं सुरेशम्
विश्वाधारं गगनसदृशं मेघवर्णं शुभाङ्गम्।
लक्ष्मीकान्तं कमलनयनं योगिभिर्ध्यानगम्यम्
वन्दे विष्णुं भवभयहरं सर्वलोकैकनाथम्॥

śhāntākāram bhujagaśhayanam padmanābhām sureśham
viśhvādhāram gaganasadṛiśham meghavarṇam śhubhāṅgam
lakśhmīkāntam kamalanayanam yogibhirdhyānagamyam
vande viṣhṇum bhavabhayaharam sarvalokaikanātham

We celebrate Lord Vishnu, who is home to serenity and peace, who rests on a bed of serpents and from whose navel a lotus stems. He is the chief of all celestial beings and the sustainer of the universe. He is infinite and endless like the skies and has a bluish complexion like the rain-bearing clouds. The Supreme Lord is the beloved of Goddess Lakshmi and possesses lotus-like eyes. Great saints meditate on Him. He removes all fears from the heart of His devotees. We bow down to the Lord, who is the Supreme Master of innumerable universes.

Kayena Vacha

कायेन वाचा मनसेन्द्रियैर्वा बुद्ध्यात्मना वा प्रकृतेः स्वभावात्।
करोमि यद्यत्सकलं परस्मै नारायणयेति समर्पयामि॥

kāyena vāchā manasendriyairvā buddhyātmanā vā prakṛiteḥ svabhāvāt
karomi yadyatsakalam parasmai nārāyaṇayeti samarpayāmi

Whatever actions we perform with our body, speech, mind, senses, intellect, soul and natural tendencies, we surrender them all to the Supreme Lord Narayan.

Lord Shiv

Karpura Gauram

कर्पूरगौरं करुणावतारं संसारसारं भुजगेन्द्रहारम्।
सदा वसन्तं हृदयारविन्दे भवं भवानीसहितं नमामि॥

karpūragauram karuṇāvatāram sansārasāram
bhujagendrahāram
sadā vasantam hṛidayāravinde bhavam bhavānīsahitam namāmi

Lord Shiv's fair complexion is anointed with camphor. He is the personification of love and kindness. The entire universe resides within Him. He wears a snake garland around His neck. We offer our respects to the Lord and Mother Parvati (Bhavani), pleading with them to reside in our hearts forever.

Mother Parvati

Sarva Mangala Mangalye

सर्वमङ्गलमाङ्गल्ये शिवे सर्वार्थसाधिके।
शरण्ये त्र्यम्बके गौरि नारायणि नमोऽस्तु ते॥

sarva-maṅgala-māṅgalye śhive sarvārtha-sādhike
śharaṇye tryambake gauri nārāyaṇi namo 'stu te

We prostrate ourselves before Mother Parvati, who is most benevolent and bestows well-being upon the world. She is the wife of Lord Shiv, sister of Lord Vishnu and the protector of all living beings—demons, humans and celestials.

Mantras

Om Gan Ganapathaye

ॐ गं गणपतये नमो नमः।
श्री सिद्धिविनायक नमो नमः।
अष्टविनायक नमो नमः।
गणपती बाप्पा मोरया॥

om̐ gan gaṇapataye namo namaḥ
śhrī siddhivināyaka namo namaḥ
aṣhṭavināyaka namo namaḥ
gaṇapatī bāppā morayā

We sing the glories of Lord Ganesh, who bestows His powers upon His devotees. He also manifests in eight different forms. Therefore, we pay our respects to Lord Ganapati—the head of the ganas (semi-divine beings who are associates of Lord Shiv).

Hare Ram Hare Krishna Mahamantra

हरे राम हरे राम राम राम हरे हरे।
हरे कृष्ण हरे कृष्ण कृष्ण कृष्ण हरे हरे॥

hare rāma hare rāma rāma rāma hare hare
hare kṛiṣhṇa hare kṛiṣhṇa kṛiṣhṇa kṛiṣhṇa hare hare

We seek the grace of the divine energy of God, Radha Rani (Harā) to attain divine love from the Supreme Almighty Shri Krishna.

Shanti Mantra

Sarveshaam Svastir Bhavatu

ॐ सर्वेषां स्वस्तिर्भवतु।
सर्वेषां शान्तिर्भवतु।
सर्वेषां पूर्णं भवतु।
सर्वेषां मङ्गलं भवतु।
ॐ शान्तिः शान्तिः शान्तिः॥

om̃ sarveṣhām svastir-bhavatu
sarveṣhām śhantir-bhavatu
sarveṣhām pūrṇam bhavatu
sarveṣhām maṅgalam bhavatu
om̃ śhāntiḥ śhāntiḥ śhāntiḥ

We pray to the Supreme Lord for the good health of all beings. We call on Him for the peace, fulfilment and prosperity of all living beings. May peace prevail.

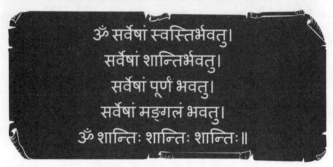

Sarve Bhavantu Sukhinah

ॐ सर्वे भवन्तु सुखिनः
सर्वे सन्तु निरामयाः।
सर्वे भद्राणि पश्यन्तु
मा कश्चिद्दुःख-भाग्भवेत्।
ॐ शान्तिः शान्तिः शान्तिः॥

om̃ sarve bhavantu sukhinaḥ
sarve santu nirāmayāḥ
sarve bhadrāṇi paśhyantu
mā kaśhchid duḥkha-bhāgbhavet
om̃ śhāntiḥ śhāntiḥ śhāntiḥ

Om! We pray to the Master of the universe for happiness, good health and well-being for one and all. We ask Him for the prevalence of peace by eradicating all suffering.

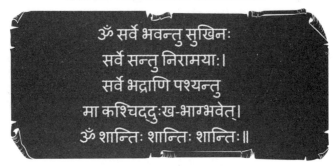

Asato Ma Sadgamaya

ॐ असतो मा सद्गमय।
तमसो मा ज्योतिर्गमय
मृत्योर्माऽमृतं गमय॥
ॐ शान्तिः शान्तिः शान्तिः॥

om̃ asato mā sadgamaya
tamaso mā jyotirgamaya
mṛityormā 'mṛitam gamaya
om̃ śhāntiḥ śhāntiḥ śhāntiḥ

Om! We pray to the Supreme Entity that He may lead everyone from untruth to truth, from darkness to light, and from death to immortality. Thus, we call on the Lord for everlasting inner peace.

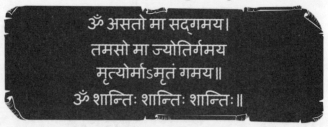

Bhajans

Gauri-Nandana Gajanana

गौरी-नन्दन गजानन
गिरिजा-नन्दन निरञ्जन।
पार्वती-नन्दन शुभानन
पाहि प्रभो मां पाहि प्रसन्न॥

gaurī-nandana gajānana
girijā-nandana nirañjana
pārvatī-nandana śhubhānana
pāhi prabho mām pāhi prasanna

We sing the glories of Lord Ganesh, son of Mother Parvati (also referred to as Gauri and Girija) and the one with an elephant face. He is pure, untainted and auspicious. We beseech Him to provide us with His protection and bliss.

Raghupati Raghav Rajaram

रघुपति राघव राजा राम,
पतित पावन सीता-राम।
सीता-राम सीता-राम,
भज प्यारे तू सीता-राम।
ईश्वर अल्लाह तेरो नाम,
सबको सन्मति दे भगवान॥

raghupati rāghava rājā rāma
patita pāvana sītā rāma
sītā rāma sītā rāma
bhaja pyāre tū sītā rāma
īśhvara allāha tero nāma
sabako sanmati de bhagavān

We sing the glories of Lord Ram. He is the Lord of the Raghu dynasty. Along with His eternal wife, Sita, He is the saviour of the fallen souls. Therefore, we constantly chant the names of Sita and Ram. The Supreme Lord is called by different names, such as 'Ishwar' and 'Allah'. We pray to the Lord to bestow wisdom on all.

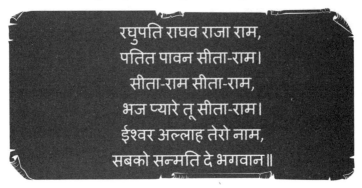

Hari Hari Bol

हरि हरि बोल, बोल हरि बोल।
मुकुन्द माधव गोविन्द बोल।
केशव माधव गोविन्द बोल।
हरि हरि बोल के ले ले हरि मोल।

hari hari bol, bol hari bol
mukunda mādhava govinda bol
keśhava mādhava govinda bol
hari hari bol ke le le hari mol

We sing the names and virtues of the Supreme Lord Hari (Shri Krishna). We chant Shri Krishna's divine names, Mukund, Madhav and Govind. We chant Shri Krishna's glorious names, Keshav, Madhav and Govind. By chanting His names, we can win over the most precious Shri Krishna without paying any price.

Om Mangalam

ॐ मङ्गलमं औंकार मङ्गलम्।
गुरु मङ्गलं गुरु पाद मङ्गलम्॥

om̃ maṅgalam omkār maṅgalam
guru maṅgalam guru pād maṅgalam

The eternal syllable 'Om' and its vibrating sound, 'Omkar', are sacred and auspicious. The Guru and His lotus feet are sacred and benign as well.

Itni Shakti Hamein Dena Daata

इतनी शक्ति हमें देना दाता
मन का विश्वास कमज़ोर हो ना।
हम चलें नेक रस्ते पे हम से
भूलकर भी कोई भूल हो ना॥ ...

दूर अज्ञान के हों अन्धेरे
तू हमें ज्ञान की रौशनी दे।
हर बुराई से बचते रहें हम
जितनी भी दे, भली ज़िन्दगी दे।
बैर हो ना किसी का किसी से
भावना मन में बदले की हो ना॥ ...

itanī śhakti hamein denā dātā
mana kā viśhvāsa kamazora ho nā
hama chalen neka raste pe hama se
bhūlakara bhī koī bhūla ho nā ...

dūra ajñāna ke hon andhere
tū hamein jñāna kī raushanī de
hara burāī se bachate rahen hama
jitanī bhī de, bhalī zindagī de
baira ho nā kisī kā kisī se
bhāvanā mana men badale kī ho nā...

O Lord! Grant us such immense strength that our faith in You remains firm. May we follow the path of truthfulness. May we not commit a mistake even unintentionally.

O Lord! Please eradicate the darkness of ignorance within us and bestow upon us the light of knowledge. May we stay protected from all evil deeds. No matter how long we live, may we live a good life. May we never view anyone as our enemy. May we never harbour sentiments of revenge towards anyone.

Wisdom Nuggets

Kindness

मूलं भुजङ्गैः शिखरं विहङ्गैः
शाखां प्लवङ्गैः कुसुमानि भृङ्गैः।
आश्चर्यमेतत् खलु चन्दनस्य
परोपकाराय सतां विभूतयः॥

mūlam bhujaṅgaiḥ śhikharam vihaṅgaiḥ
śhākhām plavaṅgaiḥ kusumāni bṛiṅgaiḥ
āśhcharyametat khalu chandanasya
paropakārāya satām vibhūtayaḥ

A sandalwood tree has many utilities. Its roots act as shelter for snakes, while birds make their nests on top of it. Its branches serve as playful spots for monkeys, while the flowers cater to honeybees. Similarly, good people offer their help to each and every one.

Respect

मातृ देवो भव।
पितृ देवो भव।
आचार्य देवो भव।
अतिथि देवो भव।

mātṛi devo bhava
pitṛi devo bhava
āchārya devo bhava
atithi devo bhava

Respect your mother as you respect God; respect your father as you respect God; respect your teacher as you respect God; respect your guests as you respect God.

Integrity

सत्यं ब्रूयात् प्रियं ब्रूयात् न ब्रूयात् सत्यमप्रियम्।
प्रियं च नानृतं ब्रूयादेष धर्मः सनातनः॥

satyam brūyāt priyam brūyāt na brūyāt satyamapriyam
priyam cha nānṛitam brūyādeṣha dharmaḥ sanātanaḥ

Speak the truth; speak pleasantly. Do not speak truth that is unpleasant to others. Even if it is pleasant, do not speak untruth. This is the path of eternal righteousness.

Perseverance

काल करे सो आज कर, आज करे सो अब।
पल में प्रलय होएगी, बहुरि करेगा कब॥

kāla kare so āja kara, āja kare so aba
pala men pralaya hoegī, bahuri karegā kaba

Whatever you plan to do tomorrow, do it today. Whatever you plan to do today, do it right now. Do not procrastinate. One can lose life in the blink of an eye.

Accountability

चिन्तनीया हि विपदामादावेव प्रतिक्रिया।
न हि कूपखननं युक्तं प्रदीप्ते वह्निना गृहे॥

chintanīyā hi vipadāmādādeva pratikriyā
na hi kūpakhananam yuktam pradīpte vahninā gṛihe

Think of the consequences of your actions before you act. It is no use digging a well after the house has caught fire.

Love

कबीरा सब जग निर्धना, धन्वन्ता नहीं कोय।
धन्वन्ता सोई जानिये, जाहि प्रेम धन होय॥

kabīrā saba jaga nirdhanā, dhanvantā nahīn koya
dhanvantā soī jāniye, jāhi prema dhana hoya

Saint Kabir says: 'In this world everybody is poor, nobody is rich. Only the one who has love for God is truly wealthy.'

Humility (Unassuming)

बड़ा हुआ तो क्या हुआ, जैसे पेड़ खजूर।
पन्थी को छाया नहीं, फल लागे अति दूर॥

baṛā huā to kyā huā, jaise peṛa khajūra
panthī ko chāyā nahīn, phala lāge ati dūra

A person's greatness is of no use if he has no humility. A date tree, though tall, does not provide shade to the birds, nor can its fruits be reached easily.

Seniors

Shlokas

The Guru

Agyana Thimirandhasya

ॐ अज्ञानतिमिरान्धस्य ज्ञानाञ्जनशलाकया।
चक्षुरुन्मीलितं येन तस्मै श्रीगुरवे नमः॥

oṁ ajñāna-timirāndhasya jñānāñjana-śhalākayā
chakṣur unmīlitam yena tasmai śhrī-gurave namaḥ

Om! We offer our humble respects to that Spiritual Master who eradicates our ignorance of infinite lifetimes with the torchlight of divine knowledge. He opens our eyes, enabling us to see the truth.

Dhyana Moolam Guror Moortih

ध्यानमूलं गुरोर्मूर्तिः पूजामूलं गुरोः पदम्।
मंत्रमूलं गुरोर्वाक्यं मोक्षमूलं गुरोः कृपा॥

dhyāna mūlam guror mūrtiḥ pūjā mūlam guroḥ padam
mantra mūlam guror vākyam mokṣha mūlam guroḥ kṛipā

The form of the Guru is the basis of meditation. His lotus feet are the starting point of all worship. The words of the Guru are the essence of all mantras. His grace is the foundation of liberation.

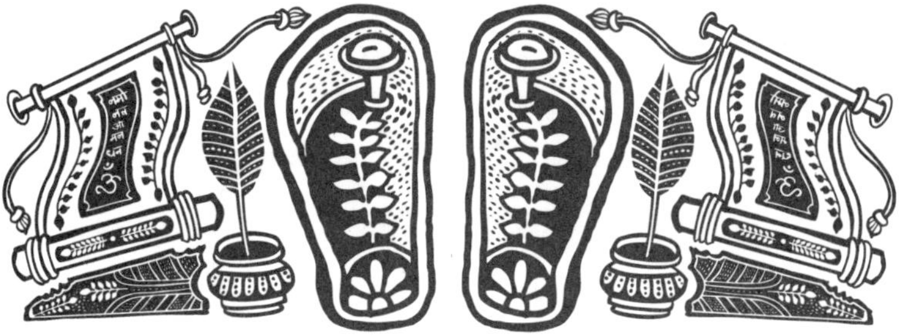

Lord Ganesh

Pranamya Shirasa Devam

प्रणम्य शिरसा देवं गौरीपुत्रं विनायकम्।
भक्तावासं स्मरेन्नित्यमायुःकामार्थसिद्धये॥

praṇamya śhirasā devam gaurī-putram vināyakam
bhaktāvāsam smaren-nityam-āyuḥ-kāma-artha-siddhaye

We bow our heads before Lord Ganesh, the son of Mother Gauri (Parvati). He is the leader of all. He dwells in the heart of His devotees. We meditate upon Him for long life, prosperity and fulfilment of desires.

Ekadantam Mahakayam

एकदन्तं महाकायं तप्त काञ्चन सन्निभम्।
लम्बोदरं विशालाक्षं वन्देऽहं गणनायकम्॥

ekadantam mahākāyam taptakāñchana sannibham
lambodaram viśhālākṣham vande 'ham gaṇanāyakam

We offer humble respects to Lord Gananayaka (Ganesh), the leader of the attendants of Lord Shiv. He is single-tusked and has a humongous body that glows like molten gold. He has a huge belly and large eyes.

Lord Krishna

Kararavindena Padaravindam

करारविन्देन पदारविन्दं मुखारविन्दे विनिवेशयन्तम्।
वटस्य पत्रस्य पुटे शयानं बालं मुकुन्दं मनसा स्मरामि॥

kara-aravindena pada-aravindam mukha-aravinde
vi-niveśhay-antam
vaṭasya patrasya puṭe śhayānam bālam mukundam
manasā smarāmi

We fondly remember the beautiful Baby Mukund (Krishna), who reclines on a banyan leaf. He holds His lotus-like feet with His soft and gentle lotus-like hands and places them in His lotus-like mouth.

Lord Ram

Apadam Apahartaram

आपदां-अपहर्तारं दातारं सर्व संपदाम्
लोकाभिरामं श्रीरामं भूयो भूयो नमाम्यहम्॥

āpadām apahartāram dātāram sarva sampadām
lokābhirāmam śhrīrāmam bhūyo bhūyo namāmyaham

We bow down and offer our prayers to Lord Ram again and again. He eradicates all obstacles from our path and blesses us with prosperity. He is the darling of the entire world.

Shuddha Brahma Paratpara Ram

शुद्ध-ब्रह्म-परात्पर-राम॥
कालात्मक-परमेश्वर-राम॥
शेष-तल्प-सुख-निद्रित-राम॥
ब्रह्माध्यमर-प्रार्थित-राम॥
राम राम जय राजा राम॥
राम राम जय सीता राम॥

śhuddha-brahma-parātpara-rāma
kālātmaka-parameśhvara-rāma
śheṣha-talpa-sukha-nidrita-rāma
brahmādhyamara-prārthita-rāma
rāma rāma jaya rājā rāma
rāma rāma jaya sītā rāma

We sing the glories of Lord Ram, who is the Supreme Almighty. He is the controller of time and destiny. He rests blissfully in yoga-nidra on the divine serpent, Ananta Shesh (as Lord Vishnu). All the gods and goddesses, including Brahma, offer their prayers to Him. May Lord Ram be victorious! May Sita and Ram be triumphant!

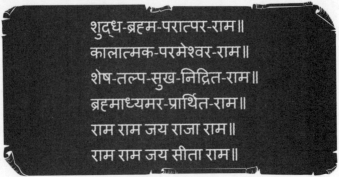

Lord Hanuman

Anjana Nandanam Veeram

अञ्जना-नन्दनं वीरं जानकी-शोकनाशनम्।
कपीशं अक्षहन्तारं वन्दे लङ्का-भयङ्करम्॥

añjanā-nandanam vīram jānakī-śhokanāśhanam
kapīśham akṣhahantāram vande laṅkā-bhayaṅkaram

We bow down with respect to Lord Hanuman, the heroic son of Anjana. He got rid of Mother Janaki's (Sita) sorrow. He is the king of monkeys. He killed Akshay Kumar (the son of Ravan) and left the residents of Lanka trembling with fear.

Atulita Bala Dhamam

अतुलितबलधामं हेमशैलाभदेहम्,
दनुजवनकृशानुं ज्ञानिनामग्रगण्यम्।
सकलगुणनिधानं वानराणामधीशम्,
रघुपतिप्रियभक्तं वातजातं नमामि॥

atulita-bala-dhāmam hema-śhailābha-deham
danuja-vana-kṛiśhānum jñāninām-agragaṇyam
sakala-guṇa-nidhānam vānarāṇām-adhīśham
raghupati-priya-bhaktam vātajātam namāmi

We salute Lord Hanuman, who possesses infinite power. His body is like a golden mountain. His strength is like a raging fire that can kill a forest of demons. He is foremost among the jnanis (the wise ones). He is the storehouse of all virtues and the master of the monkeys. He is an ardent devotee of Shri Ram and the son of wind god.

Lord Vishnu

Vanamali Gadi Sharngi

वनमाली गदी शार्ङ्गी शङ्खी चक्री च नन्दकी।
श्रीमान्नारायणो विष्णुर्वासुदेवोऽभिरक्षतु॥

vanamālī gadī śhārṅgī śhaṅkhī chakrī cha nandakī
śhrīmān nārāyaṇo viṣhṇur vāsudevo 'bhirakṣhatu

The Supreme Lord Narayan (Vishnu) is adorned with an attractive flower garland, a mace called Kaumodaki, the bow called Sharnga, the conch called Panchjanya, the sacred disc called Sudarshan Chakra and the sword called Nandaki. May all-pervading Lord Vasudev protect us.

Yasya Smarana Matrena

यस्य स्मरण मात्रेण जन्म संसार बन्धनात्।
विमुच्यते नमस्तस्मै विष्णवे प्रभविष्णवे॥

yasya smaraṇa-mātreṇa janma-sansāra-bandhanāt
vimuchyate namas-tasmai viṣhṇave prabhaviṣhṇave

We offer our salutations to Lord Vishnu, the all-powerful Lord. Just the thought of Him releases one from the bondage of the cycle of birth and death.

Mother Saraswati

Namaste Sharade Devi

नमस्ते शारदे देवि काश्मीरपुर वासिनि।
त्वामहं प्रार्थये नित्यं विद्यादानं च देहि मे॥

namaste śhārade devi kāśhmīra pura vāsini
tvām aham prārthaye nityam vidyā dānam cha dehi me

We offer our salutations to Mother Saraswati, who resides in the divine land of Kashmir. We pray to Her daily to bestow divine knowledge upon us.

Ya Kundendu

या कुन्देन्दुतुषारहारधवला या शुभ्रवस्त्रावृता
या वीणावरदण्डमण्डितकरा या श्वेतपद्मासना।
या ब्रह्माच्युत शङ्कर प्रभृतिभिर्देवैः सदा वन्दिता
सा मां पातु सरस्वती भगवती निःशेषजाड्यापहा॥

yā kundendu-tuṣhāra-hāra-dhavalā yā shubhra-vastrāvṛitā
yā vīṇā-vara-daṇḍa-maṇḍita-karā yā śhveta-padmāsanā
yā brahmāchyuta-śhaṅkara-prabhṛtibhir devaiḥ sadā vanditā
sā mām pātu sarasvatī bhagavatī niḥśheṣha-jādyāpahā

We offer salutations to Mother Saraswati, who is fair-complexioned like the jasmine flower. She is dressed in pure white clothes and wears a necklace that is as white as snow. Her hands are adorned with a veena and a boon-giving staff. She is seated on a pure white lotus. She is worshipped by Brahma, Vishnu, Shiv and all the devatas. We pray to Her to remove our ignorance and protect us.

Bhagavad Gita

Paritranaya Sadhunaam

परित्राणाय साधूनां विनाशाय च दुष्कृताम्।
धर्मसंस्थापनार्थाय सम्भवामि युगे युगे॥ 4.8॥

paritrāṇāya sādhūnām vināśhāya cha duṣhkṛitām
dharma-sansthāpanārthāya sambhavāmi yuge yuge

Lord Krishna says, 'I descend upon this earth, age after age, to protect the righteous, to destroy evil and to re-establish the principles of dharma.'

Karmanyeva Adhikaraste

कर्मण्येवाधिकारस्ते मा फलेषु कदाचन।
मा कर्मफलहेतुर्भूर्मा ते सङ्गोऽस्त्वकर्मणि॥ 2.47॥

karmaṇy-evādhikāras te mā phaleṣhu kadāchana
mā karma-phala-hetur bhūr mā te saṅgo 'stvakarmaṇi

Shri Krishna says, 'You have a right to perform your prescribed duties, but you are not entitled to the fruits of your actions. Never consider yourself to be the cause of the results of your activities, or be attached to inaction.'

Yat Karoshi

यत्करोषि यदश्नासि यज्जुहोषि ददासि यत्।
यत्तपस्यसि कौन्तेय तत्कुरुष्व मदर्पणम्॥ 9.27॥

yat karoṣhi yad aśhnāsi yaj juhoṣhi dadāsi yat
yat tapasyasi kaunteya tat kuruṣhva mad-arpaṇam

Shri Krishna says, 'Whatever you do, whatever you eat, whatever you offer to the sacred fire, whatever you bestow as a gift and whatever austerities you perform, O son of Kunti, do them as an offering to Me.'

Tasmat Sarveshu

तस्मात्सर्वेषु कालेषु मामनुस्मर युध्य च।
मय्यर्पितमनोबुद्धिर्मामेवैष्यस्यसंशयम्॥ 8.7॥

tasmāt sarveṣhu kāleṣhu mām anusmara yudhya cha
mayyarpita-mano-buddhir mām evaiṣhyasyasanśhayam

Shri Krishna says, 'Always remember Me and execute your duty of fighting the war. Surrendering your mind and intellect to Me, you will attain Me; of this, there is no doubt.'

Mantras

Gananam Tva Ganapatim Havamahe

गणानां त्वा गणपतिं हवामहे
कविं कवीनामुपमश्रवस्तमम्।
ज्येष्ठराजं ब्रह्मणां ब्रह्मणस्पत
आ नः शृण्वन्नूतिभिः सीद सादनम्॥

gaṇānām tvā gaṇapatim havāmahe
kavim kavīnāmupamaśhravastamam
jyeṣhṭharājam brahmaṇām brahmaṇas pata
ā naḥ śhṛiṇvannūtibhiḥ sīda sādanam

We offer sacrificial offerings to You, O Ganapati! You are the chief of all the ganas (associates of Lord Shiv). You are the wisdom of the wise. Your glory is well-known. You are the king of all the prayers. Listening to our prayers, kindly be present in the seat of this sacred altar (to charge our prayers with Your power and wisdom).

Maha Mrityunjaya Mantra

ॐ त्रयम्बकं यजामहे सुगन्धिं पुष्टिवर्धनम्।
उर्वारुकमिव बन्धनान् मृत्योर्मुक्षीय माऽमृतात्॥

oṁ trayambakam yajāmahe sugandhim puṣhṭivardhanam
urvārukamiva bandhanān mṛityormukṣhīya mā 'mṛitāt

We worship the three-eyed Lord Shiv. He enhances the sweetness and fragrance of life and cultivates prosperity. He can free us from the bondage of life and death as easily as a pumpkin would get detached from the mother plant. We pray to Him to free us from the cycle of life and death and grant immortality.

Shanti Mantra

Om Sahanavavatu

ॐ सह नाववतु।
सह नौ भुनक्तु॥
सह वीर्यं करवावहै।
तेजस्वि नावधीतमस्तु॥
मा विद्विषावहै।
ॐ शान्तिः शान्तिः शान्तिः॥

oṁ saha nāvavatu
saha nau bhunaktu
saha vīryam karavāvahai
tejasvi nāvadhītamastu
mā vidviṣhāvahai
oṁ śhāntiḥ śhāntiḥ śhāntiḥ

Om! May the Lord protect us (the teacher and the students) together; may He nourish us together; may He make our learning enlightening; may we not hate each other. Om! Let there be peace, peace, peace.

Purnamadah Purnamidam

ॐ पूर्णमदः पूर्णमिदं
पूर्णात् पूर्णमुदच्यते
पूर्णस्य पूर्णमादाय
पूर्णमेवावशिष्यते॥
ॐ शान्तिः शान्तिः शान्तिः

om̐ pūrṇamadaḥ pūrṇamidam
pūrṇāt pūrṇam udachyate
pūrṇasya pūrṇam ādāya
pūrṇam evāvaśhiṣhyate
om̐ śhāntiḥ śhāntiḥ śhāntiḥ

Om! The Supreme Divine is perfect and complete in all ways. The world that has emerged from Him is also flawless and complete. The Lord is so wholly complete that what has arisen from Him is complete and what remains is also whole. Om! Let there be peace, peace, peace.

Om Bhadram Karnebhih

ॐ भद्रं कर्णेभिः शृणुयाम देवाः।
भद्रं पश्येमाक्षभिर्यजत्राः।
स्थिरैरङ्गैस्तुष्टुवाँसस्तनूभिः।
व्यशेम देवहितं यदायुः॥
स्वस्ति न इन्द्रो वृद्धश्रवाः।
स्वस्ति नः पूषा विश्ववेदाः।
स्वस्ति नस्ताक्ष्र्यो अरिष्टनेमिः।
स्वस्ति नो बृहस्पतिर्दधातु॥
ॐ शान्तिः शान्तिः शान्तिः॥

oṁ bhadram karṇebhiḥ śhṛiṇuyāma devāḥ
bhadram paśhyemākṣhabhiryajatrāḥ
sthirairaṅgaistuṣhṭuvāṅgsastanūbhiḥ
vyaśhema devahitam yadāyuḥ
svasti na indro vṛiddhaśhravāḥ
svasti naḥ pūṣhā viśhvavedāḥ
svasti nastārkṣhyo ariṣhṭanemiḥ
svasti no bṛihaspatirdadhātu
oṁ śhāntiḥ śhāntiḥ śhāntiḥ

We pray to the Lord that we may hear with our ears that which is auspicious. May we see with our eyes that which is auspicious. With steady sense organs and our body held in prayer, may we attain the lifespan allotted by the devatas (and thus find fulfilment in our lives). May Indra, whose glory is great, bestow well-being upon us. May Pushan, who is all-knowing, bestow well-being upon us. May Garud, who has a ring of protection, bestow well-being upon us. May Brihaspati, Guru of the celestial gods, bestow well-being upon us. Om! Let there be peace, peace, peace.

Dhanvantari Stotram

ॐ नमो भगवते महासुदर्शनाय वासुदेवाय धन्वन्तरायेः
अमृतकलश हस्ताय सर्व भयविनाशाय सर्व रोगनिवारणाय।
त्रिलोकपथाय त्रिलोकनाथाय श्री महाविष्णुस्वरूप
श्रीधन्वन्तरी स्वरूप श्री श्री श्री औषधचक्र नारायणाय नमः॥

om̃ namo bhagavate mahāsudarśhanāya vāsudevāya dhanvantarāyeḥ
amṛitakalaśha hastāya sarva bhayavināśhāya sarva roganivāraṇāya
trilokapathāya trilokanāthāya śhrī mahāviṣhṇusvarūpa
śhrīdhanvantarī svarūpa śhrī śhrī śhrī auṣhadhachakra nārāyaṇāya namaḥ

We pay our respects to the most revered Lord Dhanvantari, also known as Vasudev and Maha-Sudarshan. He holds the pot of divine nectar in His hand and destroys fear from the hearts of people. He is the reliever of all diseases and the rescuer of the diseased. He traverses the three worlds and is the Lord of them all. Salutations to Shri Dhanvantari, who is a form of Maha-Vishnu and is worshipped as the Lord of medicines. He is gifted with the splendour and the spectrum of medicines.

Bhajans

Natwar Nagar Nanda

नटवर नागर नन्दा भजो रे मन गोविन्दा।
राधे गोविन्दा भजो राधे गोविन्दा।
वृन्दावन चन्दा भजो, वृन्दावन चन्दा।
बाल मुकुन्दा भजो, बाल मुकुन्दा।
यशोदा के नन्दा भजो, यशोदा के नन्दा॥

naṭavara nāgara nandā bhajo re mana govindā
rādhe govindā bhajo rādhe govindā
vṛindāvana chandā bhajo, vṛindāvana chandā
bāla mukundā bhajo, bāla mukundā
yaśhodā ke nandā bhajo, yaśhodā ke nandā

O my mind! Chant and glorify the name of Govind, who is the best among the rasiks and is enchanting like a charming prince. Sing the glories of Radha and Govind. Chant the praises of Shri Krishna, the moon of Vrindavan. Glorify Baby Mukund, the childhood form of Shri Krishna. Sing songs of the splendour of Yashoda's darling son, Shri Krishna.

Govind Bolo Hari Gopal Bolo

गोविन्द बोलो हरि गोपाल बोलो।
राधा रमण हरि गोविन्द बोलो॥

govinda bolo hari gopāla bolo
rādhā ramaṇa hari govinda bolo

Chant the glorious names of God—Govind (He who is pleasing to the senses) and Gopal (He who takes care of the cows). Chant the divine names of Shri Krishna who is the beloved of Radha Rani.

Bhajo Giridhar Govind Gopala

भजो गिरिधर गोविन्द गोपाला
भजो मुरली मनोहर नन्दलाला
कृष्ण गोविन्द गोविन्द गोपाला
भजो गोपाला गोपाला भजो गोपाला

bhajo giridhara govinda gopālā
bhajo murali manohara nandalālā
kṛiṣhṇa govinda govinda gopālā
bhajo gopālā gopālā bhajo gopālā

Chant the divine names of Lord Krishna—Giridhar (He who lifted the Govardhan hill), Govind and Gopal. Chant the praises and glories of the son of Nand (Shri Krishna) who captivates everyone's heart by playing His divine flute. Chant the names and glories of Shri Krishna. Chant the name and virtues of Gopal.

Hey Sharade Ma

हे शारदे माँ, हे शारदे माँ
अज्ञानता से हमें तार दे माँ।

तू स्वर की देवी, ये संगीत तुझसे,
हर शब्द तेरा, है हर गीत तुझसे,
हम हैं अकेले, हम हैं अधूरे,
तेरी शरण हम, हमें प्यार दे माँ।

मुनियों ने समझी, गुणियों ने जानी,
वेदों की भाषा, पुराणों की बानी,
हम भी तो समझें, हम भी तो जानें,
विद्या का हमको अधिकार दे माँ।

तू श्वेतवर्णी, कमल पर विराजे,
हाथों में वीणा, मुकुट सर पे साजे,
मन से हमारे मिटा के अन्धेरे,
हमको उजालों का संसार दे माँ।

हे शारदे माँ, हे शारदे माँ,
अज्ञानता से हमें तार दे माँ।

he śhārade māñ, he śhārade māñ
ajñānatā se hamen tāra de māñ

tū svara kī devī, ye sangīta tujhase,
hara śhabda terā, hai hara gīta tujhase,
hama hain akele, hama hain adhūre,
terī śharaṇa hama, hamen pyāra de māñ

muniyon ne samajhī, guṇiyon ne jānī,
vedon kī bhāṣhā, purāṇon kī bānī
hama bhī to samajhen, hama bhī to jānen
vidyā kā hamako, adhikāra de māñ

tū śhvetavarṇī, kamala para virāje
hāthon men vīṇā, mukuṭa sara pe sāje
mana se hamāre miṭāke andhere
hamako ujālon kā sansāra de māñ

he śhārade māñ, he śhārade māñ
ajñānatā se hamen tāra de māñ

O Mother Saraswati! Help us cross over the ocean of ignorance.

O Mother Saraswati! You are the Goddess of music. You are the song of life. Every word of ours is in praise of You. We sing Your glories alone. We are lonely and incomplete without You. We seek refuge at Your lotus feet. O Mother, please shower Your love upon us.

The sages and the righteous people have known and understood Vedic wisdom. Please bless us as well with the knowledge of the scriptures.

You wear white robes. You are seated on a lotus, holding the veena. Your head is embellished with a beautiful crown. O Mother, please eradicate the darkness in our heart and place us in the light of knowledge.

O Mother Saraswati! Help us cross over this ocean of ignorance.

Vaishnav Jana To

वैष्णव जन तो तेने कहिये जे, पीड परायी जाणे रे ।
पर दुःखे उपकार करे तो ये, मन अभिमान न आणे रे ॥

सकळ लोकमां सहुने वंदे, निंदा न करे केनी रे ।
वाच काछ मन निश्चल राखे, धन धन जननी तेनी रे ॥

समदृष्टि ने तृष्णा त्यागी, परस्त्री जेने मात रे ।
जिह्वा थकी असत्य न बोले, परधन नव झाले हाथ रे ॥

मोह माया व्यापे नहि जेने, दृढ़ वैराग्य जेना मनमां रे ।
रामनाम शुं ताळी रे लागी, सकळ तीरथ तेना तनमां रे ॥

वणलोभी ने कपटरहित छे, काम क्रोध निवार्या रे ।
भणे नरसैय्यो तेनुं दरसन करतां, कुळ एकोतेर तार्या रे ॥

vaiṣhṇava jana to tene kahiye je, pīḍa parāyī jāṇe re
para duḥkhe upakāra kare toye, mana abhimāna na āṇe re

sakaḷa loka mān sahune vande, nindā na kare kenī re
vācha-kāchha mana niśhchala rākhe, dhana-dhana jananī tenī re

sama-dṛiṣhṭi ne tṛiṣhṇā tyāgī, para-strī jene māta re
jihvā thakī asatya na bole, para-dhana nava jhāle hātha re

moha-māyā vyāpe nahi jene, dṛiṛha-vairāgya jenā manamān re
rāma-nāma śhun tāḷī re lāgī, sakaḷa tīratha tenā tanamān re

vaṇa-lobhī ne kapaṭa-rahita che, kāma krodha nivāryā re
bhaṇe narasaiyyo tenun darasana karatān, kuḷa ekotera tāryā re

Devotees of the Lord are those who understand and feel other's pain. They are ever ready to help people in need. Yet, they never allow pride to overpower them.

Devotees of the Lord tolerate all disrespect. In turn, they respect every living being. They neither complain nor find faults in others. Their speech is always pure and sublime. Their mothers are blessed to have given birth to such noble children.

Devotees of the Lord are without prejudice and worldly desires. They view every woman, apart from their wife, as their mother. Their tongue refrains from telling lies. They do not even touch another's wealth and possessions.

Devotees of the Lord are untouched by worldly temptations because their mind is in complete control. They are totally detached from the world. As soon as they hear the name of Lord Ram, they clap their hands and rejoice in bliss. All holy places and pilgrimages reside in their mind.

Devotees of the Lord are devoid of greed, lust, pretence and anger. The poet Narsi Mehta thus says, 'I wish to meet such a Vaishnav, for by his virtue my entire family shall attain God.'

Wisdom Nuggets

Kindness

प्रियवाक्यप्रदानेन सर्वे तुष्यन्ति जन्तवः।
तस्मात्तदेव वक्तव्यं वचने का दरिद्रता॥

priyavākyapradānena sarve tuṣhyanti jantavaḥ
tasmāttadeva vaktavyam vachane kā daridratā

Using kind words makes everyone happy. There is no dearth of soft and gentle words. Therefore, always speak politely.

Respect

गुणी गुणं वेत्ति न वेत्ति निर्गुणो बली बलं वेत्ति न वेत्ति निर्बलः।
पिको वसन्तस्य गुणं न वायसः करी च सिंहस्य बलं न मूषकः॥

guṇī guṇam vetti na vetti nirguṇo balī balam vetti na vetti nirbalaḥ
piko vasantasya guṇam na vāyasaḥ karī cha sinhasya balam na mūṣhakaḥ

Only good people can appreciate goodness in others. Those devoid of virtues cannot see it in others. Only the strong can truly acknowledge the strength of others, while the weak cannot. Just as the cuckoo appreciates the advent of the spring season and not the crow, and an elephant understands the might of a lion and not a mouse.

Integrity

एको धर्मः परं श्रेयः क्षमैका शान्तिरुत्तमा।
विद्यैका परमा दृष्टिरहिंसैका सुखावहा॥

eko dharmaḥ param śhreyaḥ kṣhamaikā śhantiruttamā
vidyaikā paramā dṛiṣhṭirahinsaikā sukhāvahā

The highest auspiciousness is attained only by following dharma. Forgiveness is the key to establishing supreme peace. Knowledge provides the best way to look at things. And true happiness results from following non-violence.

Perseverance

उद्यमेनैव हि सिध्यन्ति कार्याणि न मनोरथैः।
न हि सुप्तस्य सिंहस्य प्रविशन्ति मुखे मृगाः॥

udyamenaiva hi sidhyanti, kāryāṇi na manorathaiḥ
na hi suptasya sinhasya, praviśhanti mukhe mṛigāḥ

Actions bear fruit only through sincere efforts and not by wishful thoughts. Animals do not enter voluntarily into the mouth of a sleeping lion.

Accountability

काव्यशास्त्रविनोदेन कालो गच्छति धीमताम्।
व्यसनेन च मूर्खाणां निद्रया कलहेन वा॥

kāvyaśhāstravinodena kālo gachchhati dhīmatām
vyasanena cha mūrkhāṇām nidrayā kalahena vā

For virtuous persons, time passes in discussions on the joys of (reading) literature and the scriptures and for fools (time is spent) in vices, wasteful sleep or quarrels.

Love

पोथी पढ़ि पढ़ि जग मुआ पण्डित भया न कोय।
ढाई आखर प्रेम का पढ़े सो पण्डित होय॥

pothī paṛhi paṛhi jaga muā, paṇḍita bhayā na koya,
ḍhāī ākhara prema kā, paṛhe so paṇḍita hoya

In reading the scriptures, life passes by, and yet no one becomes a scholar. But those who learn the secret of the two-and-a-half syllables of '*prem*' (love), are truly wise.

Humility (Unassuming)

तृणानि नोन्मूलयति प्रभन्जनो मृदुनि नीचैः प्रणतानि सर्वतः।
स्वभाव एवोन्नतचेतसामयं महान्महत्स्वेव करोति विक्रमम् ॥

tṛiṇāni nonmūlayati prabhanjano mṛiduni nīchaiḥ praṇatāni sarvataḥ
svabhāva evonnatachetasāmayam mahānmahatsveva karoti vikramam

A storm destroys only the huge and unbending trees. It does not harm the soft and tender grass. This is also the nature of noble people. The great and the heroic show their valour only against the strong.

Other Shlokas, Mantras and Bhajans You Like

Guide to Hindi Pronunciation

अ	*a*	as *u* in b*u*t
आ	ā	as *a* in f*a*r
इ	*i*	as *i* in p*i*n
ई	*ī*	as *i* in mach*i*ne
उ	*u*	as *u* in p*u*sh
ऊ	*ū*	as *o* in m*o*ve
ए	*e*	as *a* in ev*a*de
ऐ	*ai*	as *a* in m*a*t; sometimes as *ai* in *ai*sle with the only difference that *a* should be pronounced as *u* in b*u*t, not as *a* in f*a*r
ओ	*o*	as *o* in g*o*
औ	*au*	as *o* in p*o*t, or as *aw* in s*aw*
ऋ	*ṛi*	as *ri* in K*ri*shna[1]
:	*ḥ*	it is a strong aspirate; also lengthens the preceding vowel and occurs only at the end of a word. It is pronounced as a final *h* sound
ं	*m/n*	nasalises and lengthens the preceding vowel and is pronounced as *n* in the French word Bo*n*.[2]

1 Across the many states of India, *ṛi* is pronounced as '*ru*' as *u in* p*u*sh. In most parts of North India, *ṛi* is pronounced as *ri* in K*ri*shna. We have used the North Indian style here.

2 For both halanth and anusvaara, only 'm' is used. For words that are nasalized (अंश - Ansh, संस्कार - Sanskar, etc.) we are using n.

ँ	˜	as *an* in R*an*chi
क	*ka*	as *k* in *k*ite
ख	*kha*	as *kh* in Ec*kh*art
ग	*ga*	as *g* in *g*oat
घ	*gha*	as *gh* in di*gh*ard
ङ	*ṅ*	as *n* in fi*n*ger
च	*cha*	as *ch* in *ch*anel
छ	*chha*	as *chh* in staun*chh*eart
ज	*ja*	as *j* in *j*ar
झ	*jha*	as *dgeh* in he*dgeh*og
ञ	*ñ*	as *n* in lu*n*ch
ट	*ṭa*	as *t* in *t*ub
ठ	*ṭha*	as *th* in ho*th*ead
ड	*ḍa*	as *d* in *d*ivine
ढ	*ḍha*	as *dh* in re*dh*ead
ण`	*ṇa*	as *n* in bur*n*t
त	*ta*	as *t* in French word ma*t*ron
थ	*tha*	as *th* in e*th*er
द	*da*	as *th* in ei*th*er
ध	*dha*	as *dh* in Bud*dh*a
न	*na*	as *n* in *n*o
प	*pa*	as *p* in *p*ink

फ	*pha*	as *ph* in up*h*ill
ब	*ba*	as *b* in *b*oy
भ	*bha*	as *bh* in a*bh*or
म	*ma*	as *m* in *m*an
य	*ya*	as *y* in *y*es
र	*ra*	as *r* in *r*emember
ल	*la*	as *l* in *l*ight
व	*va*	as *v* in *v*ine, as *w* in s*w*an
श	śha	as *sh* in *sh*ape
स	*sa*	as *s* in *s*in
ष	*ṣha*	as *sh* in *sh*ow
ह	*ha*	as *h* in *h*ut
क्ष	*kṣha*	as *ksh* in frea*ksh*ow
ज्ञ	*jña*	as *gy* in bi*gy*oung
ऽ	'	
ड़	*ṛa*	There is no sign in English to represent the sound ड़ It has been written as *ṛa* but the tip of the tongue quickly flaps down.
ढ़	*ṛha*	There is no sign in English to represent the sound ढ़ It has been written as *ṛha* but the tip of the tongue quickly flaps down.
ॠ	*ṝ*	*as ree in* spree

Other Children's Books by the Author

Essence of Hinduism

Festivals of India

Healthy Body, Healthy Mind—Yoga for Children

Inspiring Stories for Children, Vol 1-4

Saints of India

Mahabharat

My Best Friend Krishna

Ramayan

An Initiative for Children by the Author

Bal-Mukund is a specially designed personality development programme for children conceptualised and mentored by Swami Mukundananda. It is a holistic programme for physical, mental, emotional and spiritual upliftment in children. Activities include yoga, pranayam, meditation, chanting of shlokas, kirtans, stories/discussion, games, language classes, interactive activities, festival celebrations and art and craft. Bal-Mukund also conducts free weekly online shloka and meditation sessions customised for children.

For more details, visit:
Website: www.bal-mukund.org
YouTube channel: 'Bal-Mukund'
Facebook: 'Bal-Mukund'
Email: balmukund@jkyog.org

Let's Connect

If you enjoyed reading this book and would like to connect with Swami Mukundananda, you can reach him through any of the following channels:

Websites: www.jkyog.org, www.jkyog.in

YouTube channels: 'Swami Mukundananda' and 'Swami Mukundananda Hindi'

Facebook: 'Swami Mukundananda' and 'Swami Mukundananda Hindi'

Instagram: 'Swami Mukundananda' and 'Swami Mukundananda Hindi'

Twitter: Swami Mukundananda (@Sw_Mukundananda)

WhatsApp Daily Inspirations: We have two broadcast lists. You are welcome to join either or both.
USA: +1 346-239-9675
India: +91 84489 41008

Email: deskofswamiji@swamimukundananda.org

To bring Swami Mukundananda to your organisation—as Google, Intel, Oracle, Verizon, United Nations, Stanford University, Yale University, IIT's and IIMs have—please write to deskofswamiji@swamimukundananda.org

About the Author

Swami Mukundananda is a global spiritual leader, authority on mind management, thought leader, Vedic scholar and a bhakti saint. He is the founder of the non-profit organisation JKYog and the author of numerous best-sellers, such as *7 Mindsets for Success, Happiness and Fulfilment, 7 Divine Laws to Awaken Your Best Self, Essence of Hinduism, The Science of Mind Management* and many more.

Swamiji graduated from the most prestigious institutes of the world, IIT and IIM. He is a senior disciple of Jagadguru Shri Kripaluji Maharaj. Having received the most priceless wisdom, Swamiji now travels the world, spreading the message of divine love and selfless service to God. He presents the most esoteric knowledge in a logical, simple and soul-nourishing style.

Swamiji tirelessly conducts programs every day of the week and yet carves out time for writing books, recording videos and podcasts, directing programmes for children and youth and conducting interactive sessions with devotees all around the globe. He has also designed various courses conducted online and in person, which help one to master the mind and also soak themselves in devotion.

In Cuttack, Odisha, on a 100-acre campus, he has established the biggest naturopathy and yoga hospital of eastern India and also a charitable allopathic hospital for villagers. The same campus houses a skill institute that empowers women and rural youth with education and employment. The Jagadguru Kripalu University is presently under construction. In the US, his headquarters is the Radha Krishna Temple of Dallas that includes the Center for Indian Culture and Education.

Swamiji continues to inspire, transform, and empower millions of souls across the globe. True to what he preaches, Swamiji is an embodiment of humility and selfless service. Keeping the same spirit alive, Swamiji presents this one-of-a-kind book for all young and amazing minds.

The red panda is a reddish-brown mammal with a long, ringed tail and a raccoon-like face. Also called a firefox, it is found in the forest of the eastern Himalayas. In India, it lives in Sikkim, Arunachal Pradesh, in the Darjeeling district of West Bengal, and parts of Meghalaya. Its diet includes bamboo shoots and leaves, grass, fruit, roots and insects. The cat-sized red panda uses its bushy tail for balance and to wrap around its body for warmth up in the mountains.The red panda is now an endangered species, with less than 10,000 left in the wild.